Homoeopathy for pets

A guide to the use of classical
homoeopathic medicines
in the treatment of common
ailments and conditions in
domestic animals

by George MacLeod

D0544080

Homoeopathy for pets

A guide to the use of classical
homoeopathic medicines
in the treatment of common
ailments and conditions in
domestic animals

First Published 1981
Fifth Edition (revised) 1993

Wigmore Publications Ltd
9 Cavendish Square
London W1M 9DD
Great Britain

© Wigmore Publications Ltd.
ISBN 0-907688-00-6

The Author

George MacLeod, M.R.C.V.S., D.V.S.M., is veterinary consultant to the Homoeopathic Development Foundation and principal of a highly successful veterinary practice in the South of England. He is one of the world's foremost authorities on the use of homoeopathic remedies for animal ailments. Over the last forty years he has treated all types of animals, from classic racehorses to small household pets—often achieving success where others failed.

A graduate of Glasgow University, George MacLeod lives in Haywards Heath, Sussex.

Recommended by

Homœopathic Development Foundation Ltd

CONTENTS

	Page
Introduction	3
What is homoeopathy?	4
How homoeopathy developed	5
Treating animals homoeopathically	6
Selecting the right medicine	7
General instructions for the use of the remedies in the home	8
List of homoeopathic remedies	9
Index of animal ailments	10-16
List of medicines and their indications	17-26
From George MacLeod's casebook	27-28

Introduction

This booklet has been prepared by the Homoeopathic Development Foundation as part of an information programme aimed at telling the general public more about homoeopathy and its value. In providing an easy-to-use guide to the treatment of common ailments and conditions in pets the Foundation believes it is fulfilling a need felt by a growing number of people. The booklet deals only briefly with the background and development of homoeopathy but it is hoped that enough basic information is provided to stimulate your interest and to encourage you to look for more.

It must be emphasised that this publication should not be regarded as a substitute for expert advice from a homoeopathic veterinary surgeon. Further, where symptoms persist beyond a reasonable period you should always consult a qualified vet. Used as a handy household reference, however, the booklet will be found to be of real help in the treatment of those simple complaints which occur in day-to-day life of our pets.

For many years classical homoeopathic medicines have been recognised as a safe and effective means of treating ailments, serious and minor, in humans and animals alike. Indeed, the principle of homoeopathy—that like cures like—has been known from the time of the ancient Greeks.

Today homoeopathy is widely recognised and is in general use throughout the world. In Britain it has been favoured by various members of the Royal Family, is recognised by Act of Parliament and is available on prescription under the National Health Service.

In recent years it has been found that homoeopathy is as effective for animals as for humans. It has been used with equal success on domestic pets, farm animals, racehorses and animals in captivity.

Classical homoeopathic medicines are:
* Widely recognised as a safe and effective alternative to conventional medicines.
* In general use throughout the world.
* Prepared to impeccable modern standards of quality from pure, natural sources.
* Completely safe.

What is homoeopathy?

Derived from the Greek word *Homoios*, meaning "like", homoeopathy is the medical practice of treating like with like; that is to say, treating an illness with a substance that produces the same symptoms as those displayed by the person who is ill. Current medical opinion takes the view that the symptoms are a direct manifestation of the illness. Homoeopathy, by contrast, sees the symptoms as the body's reaction against the illness as it attempts to overcome it, and seeks to simulate and not suppress this reaction.

Homoeopathy is essentially a natural healing process, providing remedies to assist the patient to regain health by stimulating the body's natural forces of recovery. It concentrates on treating the patient, rather than the disease.

One of the principles of homoeopathy is that people vary in their response to an illness according to their basic temperament. It follows, therefore, that a homoeopath does not automatically prescribe a specific remedy for a specific illness. Instead, he tries to determine the patient's temperament and responses and so prescribe on a more individual basis. Patients suffering from the same diseases often require different remedies. On the other hand, another group of patients, with different diseases, may all benefit from the same remedy.

How homoeopathy developed

The principle of homoeopathy has been known since the time of Hippocrates, the Greek founder of medicine, around 450 B.C. More than a thousand years later the Swiss alchemist Paracelsus employed the same system of healing based upon the principle that "like cures like".

But it was not until the late 18th century that homoeopathy as it is practised today was evolved. The great German physician, scholar and chemist, Samuel Hahnemann, was chiefly responsible. Appalled by existing medical practices, he set about using the homoeopathic principle to develop an alternative which was safe, gentle and effective.

Hahnemann found that by taking small doses of cinchona bark he could produce in himself mild symptoms of malaria. If similar doses were given to people actually suffering from malaria, they were cured. The cinchona seemed to trigger a reflex in the body which helped it to cure itself.

Samuel Hahnemann eventually catalogued over 200 remedies drawn from vegetable, animal, mineral and, more rarely, biological materials. All of these were "proved" by Hahnemann and his colleagues as substances which could cure patients suffering from similar symptoms. Some of the results were quite remarkable.

The next step was to find the smallest effective dose so that the risk of side effects could be minimised. At this stage of his work Hahnemann uncovered surprising but totally conclusive evidence that the more the remedy was diluted the more effective it became. He was thus able to establish the three principles of homoeopathy:

A medicine which in large doses produces the symptoms of a disease will in small doses cure that disease;

By extreme dilution, the medicine's curative properties are enhanced and all the poisonous side effects are lost;

Homoeopathic medicines are prescribed by the study of the whole individual and according to basic temperament.

Treating animals homoeopathically

Animals in general respond well to homoeopathy. Homoeopathic treatment is used effectively for domestic pets, including cats, dogs, rabbits, tortoises, birds, hamsters and guinea pigs. It is not surprising, for this system of healing has long been recognised as extremely effective in the treatment of human beings. Not only is homoeopathy a proven alternative to conventional medicine—it is equally known to be without unpleasant or dangerous side effects and entirely safe, even for babies and young animals.

Some people have tried to explain homeopathy's success by suggesting that its effectiveness depends on the psychology of the patient, that people believe they are going to be cured and so their minds condition their bodies to respond.

This obviously cannot be true of animals. Neither can an animal assist the vet by telling him how it feels. Diagnoses must be made on the basis of observation by the practitioner and by the owner. A caring owner will usually come to know an animal's temperament and habits and will notice if, for example, it shows fear under certain conditions, has a preference for warmth or cold, or reacts in a distinctive way to strangers or other animals. All such information is important in deciding on the necessary treatment.

Given that an owner knows an animal well, it is perfectly feasible for minor ailments and conditions to be cleared up safely and simply at home using one or other of the homoeopathic remedies now available.

As with orthodox medicines for the treatment of humans, veterinary preparations—especially since the inception of the "antibiotic age"—have tended to concentrate on the destruction of bacteria in the quest for a cure. Homoeopathy rejects this all too narrow approach and attempts to treat its patient, human or animal, as a whole.

As subjective symptoms are absent (i.e. those not obvious to the observer) the homoeopathic practitioner must rely on what is known as pathological prescribing viz. his knowledge of the changes (in e.g. the liver in hepatitis or the lungs in pneumonia) enables him to prescribe a remedy which in its cruder state could cause such symptoms.

Selecting the right medicine

The treatment of animals with homoeopathic medicines is relatively straightforward. The medicines guide which follows is in two parts. The first part is an alphabetical list of symptoms and complaints and reference should be made to this first. The second part is a list of medicines. By cross reference between the two lists the appropriate medicine may be selected. Thus to select a remedy correctly:

1. Consult the Index of Ailments to find the medicines recommended for the principal symptoms.

2. Study the description of the medicines in the List of Medicines.

3. Select the medicine which most closely matches the total symptoms picture.

If there is no improvement after about a week of using the medicine then stop giving it and make a second choice by selecting another medicine which closely matches the symptoms.

General instructions for the use of the remedies in the home

Homoeopathic remedies are made in different potencies: that is to say the basic or "mother" tincture is processed in the laboratory to varying potencies. Remedies are available in a number of potencies but, **generally speaking the 6C potency is recommended for the home treatment of pets.**

How to give treatment
The ideal method of adminstration is to empty the remedy directly on the tongue when the animal is not feeding. For this purpose tablets can be crushed to a powder. However, if the animal resists, the remedy can be concealed in a small piece of bread or meat, or the crushed tablet dissolved in milk or drinking water. Difficult cats often need this approach. All medicines should be given in tablet form unless otherwise stated.

Dosage
Dosage in acute conditions may necessitate frequent repetition of the remedy, e.g., one dose every hour for three or four doses. Less frequent repetition is related to less acute conditions, e.g., one per day, or one night and morning for a few days. Chronic conditions may require treatment only once per week or less often For best results, do not handle the tablets directly. Use the container cap as a dispenser. When necessary, crush the tablets between two spoons.

Serious conditions
For more serious conditions, it is strongly recommended that a qualified veterinary surgeon be consulted.

Storage of remedies
Medicines should be stored in a cool, dry place away from light and strong-smelling substances such as camphor, disinfectants, etc. Stored properly, remedies will keep their potency for many years.

Mother tinctures
For external application, mother tinctures (∅) should be diluted to a proportion of one drop to at least ten drops of water. If this mixture proves to be too astringent, dilute further. For eye treatment, dilute one drop of mother tincture in half a tumbler of water which has been boiled and allowed to cool.

Important. Mother tinctures must never be applied to the eyes in undiluted form.

List of Homoeopathic Medicines

1 Aconitum napellus (**Aconite**)

2 Actaea racemosa (**Actaea rac.**)

3 Apis mellifica (**Apis mel.**)

4 Argentum Nitricum (**Argent. Nit.**)

5 Arnica montana (**Arnica**)

6 Arsenicum Album (**Arsen. Alb.**)

7 Belladonna (**Belladonna**)

8 Bryonia alba (**Bryonia**)

9 Calcarea Carbonica (**Calc. Carb.**)

10 Calcarea Fluorica (**Calc. Fluor**)

11 Calcarea Phosphorica (**Calc. Phos.**)

12 Cantharis vesicatoria (**Cantharis**)

13 Carbo Vegetabilis (**Carbo Veg.**)

14 Cuprum Metallicum (**Cuprum Met.**)

15 Drosera rotundifolia (**Drosera**)

16 Euphrasia officinalis (**Euphrasia**)

17 Ferrum Phosphoricum (**Ferr. Phos.**)

18 Gelsemium sempervirens (**Gelsemium**)

19 Graphites (**Graphites**)

20 Hamamelis virginica (**Hamamelis**)

21 Hepar Sulphuris (**Hepar Sulph.**)

22 Hypericum perforatum (**Hypericum**)

23 Ignatia amara (**Ignatia**)

24 Ipecacuanha (**Ipecac.**)

25 Kalium Bichromicum (**Kali. Bich.**)

26 Kalium Phosphoricum (**Kali. Phos.**)

27 Lycopodium clavatum (**Lycopodium**)

28 Mercurius Solubilis (**Merc. Sol.**)

29 Natrum muriaticum (**Nat. mur.**)

30 Nux vomica (**Nux vom.**)

31 Phosphorus (**Phosphorus**)

32 Pulsatilla nigricans (**Pulsatilla**)

33 Rhus toxicodendron (**Rhus tox.**)

34 Ruta graveolens (**Ruta grav.**)

35 Sepia (**Sepia**)

36 Silicea (**Silicea**)

37 Sulphur (**Sulphur**)

38 Thuja occidentalis (**Thuja**)

Note

These remedies may be obtained from most leading chemists and health food stores throughout the country.

Index of animal ailments

Abdomen	Bloated with audible rumbling	Lycopodium
Abrasions	For unbroken skin	Arnica
	For broken skin	Hypericum
	(Also bathe affected area with solution of Hypercal Tincture. See general instructions)	
Abscess	Acute, with inflammation and sensitivity to touch	Hepar Sulph.
	Chronic	Silicea
	Mouth Abscesses	Merc. Sol.
Aggression	Aggressive behaviour	Belladonna
Alopecia	In chilly animals who hug the fire	Arsen. Alb.
	Where the animal is eating less than usual	Lycopodium
	Where the skin is dry and cracked	Nat. Mur.
Anaemia	For constitutional states	Silicea
	For accompanying gastro-intestinal symptoms	Arsen. Alb.
	For accompanying fatness	Calc. Phos.
Anal Glands	For acute inflammation	Hepar Sulph.
	For chronic states	Silicea
	(also apply Calendula Healing Ointment)	
Appetite	Lack of, for simple digestive upsets	Carbo Veg.
	Lack of, with constipation	Nux vom.
	Animal appears to want food but rejects	Arsen. Alb.
	Depraved: In fat animals	Calc. Carb.
	In lean animals	Calc. Phos.
	Excessive, varies greatly to complete loss of appetite	Ferr. Phos.
Arthritis	Worse from movement followed by improvement on further exercise	Rhus. tox.
	With much swelling	Apis Mel.
	If the joints are bruised	Arnica
	Where bone is affected	Calc. Fluor.
	Worse for exercise	Bryonia
Bad Breath	Due to decayed teeth, accumulation of tartar, or worms – consult veterinary surgeon	
	Before appointment and to help heal extraction	Arnica
	Due to gastric upsets	Carbo Veg.
	With constipation	Nux vom.
	Following stress	Kali. Phos.
Balanitis (inflammation of the penis)	Simple, uncomplicated cases	Merc. Sol.
	Externally, use solution of Hypercal Tincture	

Bereavement	Loss of litter	Ignatia
Biliousness	After eating	Nux vom.
	With accompanying kidney involvement	Apis Mel.
	For chronic cases	Lycopodium
	For accompanying jaundice	Merc. Sol.
Bites (see also Insect bites)	Punctured On surface, bathe with solution of Hypercal Tincture	Hypericum
Bleeding Gums	See casebook	
Blinking	Frequent, often with discharge from the eyes	Euphrasia
Breath	See Bad Breath	
Bruises	Superficial	Arnica
	Deeper bruises	Ruta grav.
	With broken skin	Hamamelis
Burns	With watery blisters	Phosphorus
	Severe blistering	Cantharis
	Most cases	Burn Ointment
Canker	See Ear Infections	
Chorea	Where symptoms are worse in the morning, but better from warmth	Actaea rac.
Colic	For acute cases	Nux vom.
	With flatulence	Argent. Nit.
Conjunctivitis	Simple, uncomplicated	Argent. Nit.
	With catarrh	Pulsatilla
	After travelling where the head has been hanging out of the car window	Euphrasia
	Where the margins of lids are red	Calc. Carb.
Constipation	Simple, uncomplicated	Carbo Veg.
	With loss of appetite	Nux vom.
	For accompanying skin disorders	Sulphur
	During pregnancy	Sepia
Convulsions	With fever	Belladonna
	Where animal appears to suffer from cramping pains	Cuprum Met.
	From loss of human contact	Ignatia
	From teething	Chamomilla Granules
Cough	Hard, dry cough	Phosphorus
	Better when at rest	Bryonia
	With retching	Drosera
	Dry spasmodic cough	Cuprum Met.
Cracks/Fissures	Especially in the folds of the limbs	Graphites
Cuts	Bathe with Hypercal Tincture solution or use Hypercal Ointment	

Cystitis	Animal frequently tries to pass water	Cantharis
Dandruff	For dry, scaly skin For red skin	Arsen. Alb. Sulphur
Diarrhoea	For watery stools For slimy, blood-stained stools In nervous animals With great debility With vomiting (Seek veterinary advice) N.B. Where diarrhoea persists for longer than 24 hours, or is accompanied by vomiting, loss of appetite or listlessness, veterinary advice should be sought without delay.	Arsen. Alb. Merc. Sol. Argent. Nit. Cuprum Met. Ipecac.
Distemper	See casebook	
Distress	See Shock	
Dysentery	Slimy stools, worse at night For accompanying vomiting See also Diarrhoea, Enteritis, Gastritis.	Merc. Sol. Ipecac.
Ear Infections	When acutely inflamed and sensitive to touch Surface of ears scaly, with scabby edges Suppurating with evil smelling discharge Associated with dry skin and watery discharge, often worse late at night Chronic cases	Hepar Sulph. Kali. Bich. Merc. Sol. Arsen. Alb. Rhus tox.
Eczema	For animals preferring cool places For chilly animals showing dry coats with thirst For dry, cracked skins For sticky discharges With burning itch and vesication	Sulphur Arsen. Alb. Nat. Mur. Graphites Cantharis
Enteritis	Simple, uncomplicated cases	Arsen. Alb.
Epilepsy	Consult veterinary surgeon	
Exhaustion	After sickness After cough Following stress	Arnica Drosera Kali. Phos.
Eyelids	Swollen, especially in animals sensitive to sudden noise Inflamed, symptoms worse when animal rises from bed Swollen, where there is catarrhal discharge	Phosphorus Rhus tox. Kali. Bich.
Eyes	Profuse watering from	Euphrasia

Fear	For the timid animal	Gelsemium
	Of noise, where sudden e.g. thunder and fireworks	Phosphorus
	General hypersensitivity to noise	Kali. Phos.
Fireworks	Where the animal shows excessive fear	Phosphorus
Flatulence	Most cases	Carbo Veg.
	Due to faulty diet	Nux vom.
	Resulting from liver disorder	Lycopodium
Fractures	Slow to heal	Calc. Phos.
	General medicine for fractures, dislocations and bone injuries	Ruta grav.
Gastritis	Where stomach contents are rejected soon after food	Phosphorus
	With accompanying diarrhoea	Arsen. Alb.
	With repeated vomiting	Ipecac.
Gums	See Bleeding Gums	
	Spongy	Merc. Sol.
	Swollen	Apis Mel.
Hairball	To help animal (usually cat) to either vomit it or pass it	Nux vom.
Hayfever	Watering eyes	Euphrasia
Heart Conditions	See veterinary surgeon	
Heat-Stroke	With great thirst	Belladonna
Hepatitis	See veterinary surgeon	
Hiccough	In young puppies	Nux vom.
	In very nervous animals	Ignatia
Homesickness	For example, in boarding kennels	Ignatia
Horse-Fly Bites	To help reduce swelling	Hypericum
Hysteria	Accompanied by fits	Belladonna
	Spasmodic attacks	Cuprum Met.
Incontinence	Where age is not a factor	Calc. Fluor.
Inflammation	See Ears, Penis, Anal Glands, Kidneys, Testicles	
Injuries	With bruising	Arnica
	Involving nerves	Hypericum
	With resulting strains	Ruta grav.
	(Consult a veterinary surgeon for all but minor injuries)	
	Chronic effects of	Hamamelis
Insect Bites	Wasps or bees	Apis Mel.
	Horse-fly bites	Hypericum
	Most cases, bathe with	Pyrethrum liquid

Insomnia	In older animals	Arsen. Alb.
Jaundice	Main remedy With clay-coloured stools With tenderness over loins	Merc. Sol. Phosphorus Lycopodium
Kidneys	Inflammation of (See Nephritis)	
Mange	Most cases Alternatively N.B. Keep animal isolated	Sulphur Arsen. Alb.
Mastitis	With great heat in affected area Followed by – Where glands feel hard Chronic conditions	Belladonna Bryonia Calc. Fluor.
Metritis (Inflammation of the uterus)	See casebook	
Muscles	Weakness of	Gelsemium
Nephritis (Inflammation of the kidney)	Acute: Very acute with swelling of kidney Where associated with sickness and skin trouble With vomiting With pale coloured urine	 Apis Mel. Arsen. Alb. Phosphorus Nat. Mur.
Nipples	Cracked and sore (Also apply Calendula Healing Ointment or Calendula Cream)	Graphites
Noise	Fear of, when sudden General hypersensitivity	Phosphorus Kali. Phos.
Nose	Bleeding from Yellow ropy catarrh	Hamamelis Kali. Bich.
Operations	To aid convalescence	Kali. Phos.
Orchitis (Inflammation of the testicles)	With extreme sensitivity to touch Where fluid is present beneath the skin (dents remain in skin if pressure is applied)	Hepar Sulph. Apis Mel.
Paralysis	Consult veterinary surgeon	
Penis (Inflammation of)	See Balanitis	
Pining	See Homesickness, Bereavement	
Pregnancy, False	Where the bitch is moody or vicious Where symptoms vary greatly	Sepia Pulsatilla
Pyometritis	See casebook	
Restlessness	With frequent change of position	Aconite

Rheumatism	Where animal improves on exercise	Rhus tox.
	Where animal prefers rest	Bryonia
	For acute conditions	Ruta grav.
	With agitation	Actaea rac.
	Following exposure to draughts	Calc. Phos.
Ringworm	With circular patches, more on body than on head	Sepia
Shock	Immediately afterwards	Aconite
	Followed by	Arnica
Show animals	Fright during show	Gelsemium
Skin Conditions	See Eczema	
Sprains	Main remedy	Rhus tox.
	Also recommended	Ruta grav.
Stiffness	Of the back and neck	Actaea rac.
Stings	See Insect Bites	
Strains	Worsen at rest, improve on movement	Rhus tox.
Swelling	Containing fluid	Apis Mel.
Teething	Main remedy	Chamomilla Granules
	Which is difficult and delayed	Calc. Carb.
	Delayed, in lean young animals	Calc. Phos.
Testicles (Inflammation of)	See Orchitis	
Thunder	Where the animal shows excessive fear	Phosphorus
Tongue	Yellow coated	Bryonia
	Dry, following stress	Kali. Phos.
Travel Sickness	With restlessness and fear	Aconite
	With vomiting	Ipecac.
Trembling, Muscular	In old animals	Kali. Phos.
	After too much exercise	Rhus tox.
Twitching	Muscular	Belladonna
Ulcers	In the mouth	Merc. Sol.
Uterus (Discharge)	See casebook	
Vomiting	Accompanied with diarrhoea (Seek veterinary advice)	Ipecac
	In thirsty animals	Merc. Sol.
	Immediately following food	Phosphorus
	After cough	Cuprum Met.

Warts	On all parts of body	Thuja
Worms	Consult veterinary surgeon	
Wounds	See Abrasions, Bites, Bruises, Cuts	

Homoeopathic medicines

Medicine/ Ailment or Condition	Remarks
(1) Aconite A remedy for fevers and inflammatory states. Complaints caused by exposure to cold dry winds Complaints caused by severe fright Shivering with cold sweats Breathing difficult Upper part of body hot while the lower parts are cold Animal shows desire for large quantities of water Animal displays acute anxiety Travel sickness Restlessness	Symptoms worsen: at midnight in a warm room in cold winds Symptoms improve: in the open air
(2) Actaea rac. Stiffness of back and neck Rheumatism Chorea Painful muscles when animal is over-exercised Where the animal appears unsettled and confused	Symptoms worsen: in the morning in cold and damp when moving Symptoms improve: with warmth
(3) Apis Mel. A remedy for inflammation or injury where there is swelling containing fluid. Arthritis with swelling Swollen gums Biliousness Insect bites Inflammation of testicles Animal seeks cold surface to lie on	Symptoms worsen: from heat when touched in closed and heated rooms after sleeping Symptoms improve: in the open air from cold bathing
(4) Argent. Nit. Nervous animals with trembling Diarrhoea Colic	Symptoms worsen: with warmth at night

Medicine/ Ailment or Condition	Remarks
Argent Nit. (cont'd)	
Much flatulence Conjunctivitis Warts Weakness in limbs	Symptoms improve: in cold fresh air
(5) Arnica A remedy for accidents and injury. Use after any injury To lessen shock Bruises Sprains Exhaustion following too much exercising After dental extraction The animal shrinks away when you try to touch it	Symptoms worsen: from touch from motion in damp, cold conditions Symptoms improve: when lying down
(6) Arsen. Alb. A remedy to use where the animal shows much fear and restlessness. Animal shows no interest in food Alopecia Chilly animals who hug the fire Temperature normal but gums and lips icy cold Insomnia in older animals Anaemia Dandruff Ear infections Eczema Enteritis Gastritis Mange	Symptoms worsen: after midnight in cold wet weather Symptoms improve: from warmth
(7) Belladonna A main fever remedy. Fever with heat, redness, pain and swelling Aggressive behaviour Convulsions Hysteria which sometimes leads to fits Mastitis Muscular twitching Inflammation in the ear Heat stroke	Symptoms worsen: from noise from touch when lying down Symptoms improve: from warmth

Medicine/
Ailment or Condition **Remarks**

(8) Bryonia

Dry mouth
Great thirst
Yellow coated tongue
Arthritis
Rheumatism
Cough
Mastitis
Animal prefers to lie still since movement
increases its discomfort
Animal also prefers to lie on the affected
part as pressure relieves symptoms

Symptoms worsen:
from any movement
from warmth

Symptoms improve:
from cold applications
from rest

(9) Calc. Carb.

A remedy for overweight sluggish animals.
Bone disorders in fat young animals
Very fat puppies
Teething delayed
Conjunctivitis
Excessive appetite

Symptoms worsen:
from cold
in damp weather
at night

Symptoms improve:
in dry weather
from warmth
while lying on affected part

(10) Calc. Fluor.

Arthritis
Incontinence
Mastitis
Brittle bones
Poor teeth

Symptoms worsen:
after rest
in damp weather

Symptoms improve:
after a little movement
from warm applications

(11) Calc. Phos.

Lean bony young animals
Delayed teething
Rheumatism following exposure to
draughts
Bone problems in leaner young animals
than those which may require Calc. Carb.
Anaemia
Depraved appetite
Fractures slow to heal

Symptoms worsen:
in cold and damp
from any change in weather

Symptoms improve:
in warm dry conditions

Medicine/
Ailment or Condition   Remarks

(12) Cantharis
A remedy to use when the animal appears   Symptoms worsen:
distressed when trying to pass urine.   from touch
The animal is seen to try to pass urine   while passing urine
unsuccessfully
Cystitis   Symptoms improve:
Acute kidney inflammation   with rubbing
Burns with blistering
The animal shrinks away from being touched
Eczema with burning itch

(13) Carbo Veg.
Simple digestive upsets which causes loss   Symptoms worsen:
of appetite   during warm damp weather
Bad breath   in the evening and at night
Constipation
Flatulence – frequent breaking of wind   Symptoms improve:
                                              on breaking wind
                                              from cold

(14) Cuprum Met.
Convulsions with the appearance of cramp   Symptoms worsen:
Hysteria   in cold air
Diarrhoea followed by exhaustion   in the evening and at night
Dry spasmodic cough
Vomiting after cough   Symptoms improve:
                                              after drinking cold water

(15) Drosera
A cough remedy.   Symptoms worsen:
Coughing with retching   from warmth
Animal appears as if something were caught   when lying down
in the throat   after midnight
Coughing attacks follow closely upon
each other   Symptoms improve:
The attacks often cause a change in   while moving
the 'voice'
The attacks can cause weakness in the
animal

(16) Euphrasia
A remedy for eye ailments.   Symptoms worsen:
Watering eyes   warm winds
Often in dogs following a car journey   when indoors
with an open window   in smoky room

20

Medicine/ Ailment or Condition	Remarks
Euphrasia (cont'd) Conjunctivitis Frequent blinking Catarrhal discharge from the eyes Hayfever	Symptoms improve: in dim light or darkness
(17) Ferr. Phos. A First-aid remedy when the animal first shows signs of being 'below par'. Excitable animals Appetite can vary enormously even to complete loss	Symptoms worsen: at night from cold Symptoms improve: in summer from warmth
(18) Gelsemium Timid animals Fright in show animals Fear can cause animal to pass urine Muscular weakness Weak and trembling limbs	Symptoms worsen: from damp from excitement Symptoms improve: in the open air after passing urine
(19) Graphites A remedy for skin conditions. Most commonly occurs in the folds of limbs or behind the ears Often with a sticky discharge Eczema Cracked and sore nipples Cracks and fissures Skin smells badly	Symptoms worsen: at night in draughts Symptoms improve: in the dark from covering up
(20) Hamamelis A remedy for the chronic effects of injuries. Venous bleeding Weakness after bleeding Bruises where the skin is broken Wounds following a fight Nosebleeds	Symptoms worsen: during the day in warm moist air Symptoms improve: in the open air

Medicine/
Ailment or Condition

Remarks

(21) Hepar Sulph.

The remedy is characterised by the extreme
sensitivity to touch where the animal could
be described as 'irritable'.
The remedy is particularly helpful in cases
of suppuration.
Any condition where pus has formed
Acute Abscess with inflammation
Inflammation of the anal glands
Excessive thirst
Ear infection with inflammation
Inflammation of the testicles

Symptoms worsen:
in cold air
when affected part is touched
in draughts

Symptoms improve:
from warmth
in damp wet weather

(22) Hypericum

A remedy to help reduce pain.
Especially useful where the part is rich in
nerves e.g. the tail
Abrasions with broken skin
Bites where the skin is punctured
Horse-Fly bites
This remedy when combined with Calendula
in Hypercal Tincture and Hypercal Ointment
gives the double benefit of healing and
pain-relief when applied externally to a
wound.

Symptoms worsen:
from cold and damp
in a closed room

Symptoms improve:
in warm dry weather
in the open air

(23) Ignatia

A remedy for the pining or homesick animal.
While the owner is away
While in boarding kennels
Give this remedy immediately should you
rescue an abandoned or ill-treated animal
Bereavement following loss of litter
Hiccough
Convulsions as a result of abandonment.

Symptoms worsen:
with loneliness

Symptoms improve:
with company

(24) Ipecac

A remedy for vomiting.
Gastritis with repeated vomiting
Dysentry
Travel sickness with vomiting
Diarrhoea with vomiting (seek veterinary
advice)
Respiratory difficulties

Symptoms worsen:
while lying down
periodically

Symptoms improve:
with pressure

Medicine/ Ailment or Condition	Remarks
(25) Kali. Bich. A remedy for catarrhal symptoms. Yellow stringy discharge Catarrhal discharge Swollen eyelids Raw or obstructed nose Ear infections	Symptoms worsen: during hot weather in the morning Symptoms improve: during cold weather
(26) Kali. Phos. A remedy for the animal which has undergone stress. Exhaustion Extreme fear of noise As an aid to convalescence following an operation Muscular trembling in old animals Bad breath Dry tongue	Symptoms worsen: from noise Symptoms improve: from warmth after nourishment
(27) Lycopodium Animal may appear hungry yet is satisfied with very little food. Biliousness Jaundice with tenderness over loins Flatulence from liver upset Bloated abdomen Audible rumbling in the abdomen Liver remedy Alopecia where the appetite is poor	Symptoms worsen: in stuffy rooms from cold from noise Symptoms improve: in fresh air
(28) Merc. Sol. Jaundice Biliousness during jaundice Vomiting in thirsty animals Dysentry with slimy stools Diarrhoea with slimy blood-stained stools Inflammation of the penis Mouth ulcers Mouth abscesses Spongy gums Ears which suppurate with a badly-smelling discharge Ears with greenish discharge	Symptoms worsen: at night in a warm room Symptoms improve: with rest

Medicine/ Ailment or Condition	Remarks

(24) Nat. Mur.
A remedy to use when the normally placid
animal bites viciously without any
discernable reason.
A remedy for kidney complaints
Nephritis
Urine very pale in colour
Eczema with a dry cracked skin
Alopecia
Animals with a scrawny lean appearance

Symptoms worsen:
while lying down
in sunshine

Symptoms improve:
in the open air

(30) Nux vom.
A remedy for digestive upsets.
Hairball
Poor appetite often accompanied by
constipation
Digestive upsets
Bad breath
Colic
Flatulence
Biliousness after feeding
Hiccough in young puppies

Symptoms worsen:
from cold
from movement

Symptoms improve:
from warmth
in the evening

(31) Phosphorus
A remedy for animals very sensitive to
sudden noise – thunder, fireworks – and
show great fear.
Hepatitis (seek veterinary advice)
Jaundice
Nephritis with vomiting
Gastritis – food is vomited as soon as it
warmed in the stomach
Hard dry cough
Burns with watery blisters
Swollen eyelids

Symptoms worsen:
in the evening
with exertion

Symptoms improve:
in the cold
with sleep

(32) Pulsatilla
A remedy which helps relieve female
animal complaints.
Placid, 'shy' animals
Symptoms tend to vary greatly
False pregnancy
Creamy discharges
Little thirst
Conjunctivitis with catarrhal symptoms

Symptoms worsen:
in the evening
from heat
sudden chilling when hot

Symptoms improve:
in the open air
after cold food and drink

24

Medicine/ Ailment or Condition	Remarks
(33) Rhus tox. A major rheumatic remedy. Use this remedy if the animal's symptoms improve with a little exercise Rheumatism Arthritis Strains Sprains Muscular trembling Eyelids inflamed Ear infections The animal's symptoms are worst when rising from its bed.	Symptoms worsen: with first movement from cold and wet during rest Symptoms improve: after a little gentle exercise during warm weather
(34) Ruta grav. A main remedy for sprains or dislocations. Acute rheumatism Deep bruising Injuries with resulting strains Fractures and bone injuries Tendon and ligament injuries	Symptoms worsen: from cold during wet weather during rest Symptoms improve: with warmth with gentle exercise
(35) Sepia A remedy for the treatment of female animal complaints. Unlike Pulsatilla the temperament is unpredictable and can be vicious. False pregnancy Animal is sensitive to cold Constipation during pregnancy Ringworm	Symptoms worsen: from cold before thunder in smoky rooms Symptoms improve: with warmth after gentle exercise after rest
(36) Silicea A remedy to use when your animal has picked up a splinter, thorn or other foreign body. Slow healing infections Abscesses Inflamed anal glands Anaemia Suited to animals which always retreat should a fight start.	Symptoms worsen: from cold in cold weather at the approach of winter Symptoms improve: with warmth

Medicine/ Ailment or Condition	Remarks
(37) Sulphur. A remedy for use in skin ailments. The animal seeks cool places in which to lie Skin appears dirty and may show red patches which the animal is seen to scratch frequently Skin smells badly Breaks wind with offensive smell Mange Eczema Dandruff Constipation	Symptoms worsen: with heat at rest Symptoms improve: in fresh air
(38) Thuja A remedy for warty growths. The animal may refuse all food in the morning After vaccination, this remedy can relieve any ill-effects May help when it is observed that the animal has never been fully well since vaccination.	Symptoms worsen: in damp air Symptoms improve: in dry conditions

From George MacLeod's casebook

Eczema

A dog had a severe red rash on its side, causing frenzied scratching. The patch was wet and the dog generally listless with dry coat. It had been treated with the usual suppressives, but to no avail. The drug chosen in this case was **Sulphur** for redness and heat of skin. The dog lived to be a good age. As it was a working dog as well as a pet, I was particularly pleased with the result, although the owner took it for granted.

Another intractable case of eczema was cured by **Cantharis**. This animal had been treated by its owner with various homoeopathic remedies, all of which appeared at the time to be indicated. **Cantharis** was my choice because of the burning itch and vesication. One dose of this drug given daily for three days, produced a permanent cure after initial aggravation.

Metritis (Inflammation of the uterus)

Chronic metritis is a common condition in bitches which have never been bred from, and is characterised by a muco-purulent, often blood-stained discharge, which I find yields to **Sepia.**

Distemper

Distemper in its many forms produces a wide variety of symptoms and conditions, the most important involving the central nervous system, usually ending up in paraplegia and/or chorea. In the former, certain homoeopathic medicines produce excellent results enabling animals which have been pronounced hopeless to walk again. Consultation with a veterinary surgeon is essential.

Paraplegia (Paralysis of the limbs)

Paraplegia in dachshunds is a common occurrence (independently of distemper) and when it occurs in the female, causes spinal weakness and tendency to prolapse with lumbar pains. I have found homoeopathic medicines which produce the desired result within a few days; in the absence of homoeopathic treatment some of these cases can drag on for a few months or more. **Ruta grav.** and **Hypericum** are indicated in this condition for both dog and bitch.

Nephritis (Inflammation of kidney)

Nephritis, acute and chronic, is of common occurrence in the dog, the former characterised by pain and swelling in the lumbar region accompanied by albuminuria, and here **Apis mel.** has proved of inestimable value. The chronic form shows gradual emaciation, thirst and corneal opacity with intermittent vomiting and anorexia. In these cases, **Nat. Mur.** may help.

Ear canker

Ear canker in the dog and cat can be a scourge to both owner and animal. In the cat, this condition frequently produces loss of balance, due to the abscess in the middle ear, and many cases have given satisfactory results when treated with **Hepar Sulphuris.**

When the condition is accompanied by evil-smelling discharge with excoriation of the outer ear and skin, I have found **Mercurius Solubilis** to be extremely effective.

A very common condition in young cats is "flu" characterised by frequent sneezing, lachrymation and gastro-enteritis, producing offensive watery diarrhoea. The worst case I have ever seen was that of an unwanted kitten, six weeks old, which was brought to me for destruction.

It had been starved for several days in the hope that it would die and by the time I saw it, it was far advanced in all the flu symptoms. When it did not die to suit the owner's convenience, I was asked to get rid of it at all costs, because of the filthy condition it was in. I took it home on the way to the surgery, and my children begged me to treat the animal.

After the administration of **Arsenicum Album** three times a day for three days, the diarrhoea had ceased and the emaciated little creature was learning to eat. It grew into a healthy hunting cat, with no trace of its history showing.

Bleeding gums

Shetland collie suffering from bleeding gums with occasional vomiting containing blood-flecked mucus. Slight cutaneous haemorrhaging also present. The remedy **Phosphorus** produced a cure in three days.

Pyometritis (Discharge from uterus)

Irish setter bitch. Discharge took the form of catarrhal and then muco-purulent material for which the remedy **Sepia** prevented any relapse. This condition consists of an inflammation affecting the lining of the womb. Discharges are first clear and then become thick and discoloured due to secondary infection. It is a common occurrence in bitches with a history of false pregnancies.

Arthritis

Labrador whose condition was worse on first movement, followed by improvement on further exercise. **Rhus tox** produced considerable easing of the condition.